THE **CLOSE TO HOME**

Survival Guide

Other Close to Home Books by John McPherson

Close to Home
One Step Closer to Home
Dangerously Close to Home
Home: The Final Frontier
The Honeymoon Is Over
The Silence of the Lamberts
Striking Close to Home

Treasury Collections

Close to Home Revisited
Close to Home Unplugged

Also from John McPherson

High School Isn't Pretty
The Adventures of Buck Felner
McPherson Goes to Church
McPherson's Marriage Album
The Get Well Book

THE CLOSE TO HOME

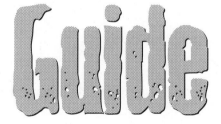

Survival Guide

A Close to Home Collection
JOHN McPHERSON

ZondervanPublishingHouse
Grand Rapids, Michigan

A Division of HarperCollinsPublishers

www.andrewsmcmeel.com

Published in cooperation with Andrews McMeel Publishing

99 00 01 02 03 BAH 10 9 8 7 6 5 4 3 2 1

ISBN: 0-310-23403-4

For Chris Millis,
an essential part of the team.

"I don't want to have to worry about you slipping in the shower again."

"Using computer-enhanced technology, these treadmills can predict how you'd look in three years if you stopped working out regularly."

With the school nurse out of the building, Todd's broken arm was cared for by the third period health class.

"Sorry folks, but at the request of other patrons, we're going to have to lower the dome of solitude."

"You're not crazy after all, Mr. Duffman! You *have* been hearing voices coming from your abdomen. Dr. Gremley's pager accidentally got sutured inside you during surgery!"

Thanks to Zach's new hydraulic pants, Linda no longer had to worry about whether a high chair was available.

"I need to have you just relax and trust me on this, Mrs. Hostrander."

Don's ant-colony shirt easily took first place at the science fair.

"The maternity nurse let me borrow the other eight. I just want to see the look on my mother's face when she walks through the door."

"Okay, let's see . . . one large pizza with pepperoni
and mushrooms . . . that'll be $9.89."

"This isn't the kind of heart-shaped
Jacuzzi I had envisioned."

"Maybe now you'll remember not to leave your gardening tools lying in the yard where someone might hit them with the mower!"

Striving to maintain her reputation as the school's most devious teacher, Mrs. Credley made her students write the 1,000-word final exam essay question on the invasion of Normandy using only candy Conversation Hearts.

"We're all out of decaf, so I stirred in
two sleeping pills."

"The bad news is that Pepper is going to need a kid-
ney transplant immediately. The good news is that,
based on our tests, you, Alan, are an ideal donor."

When teachers telecommute.

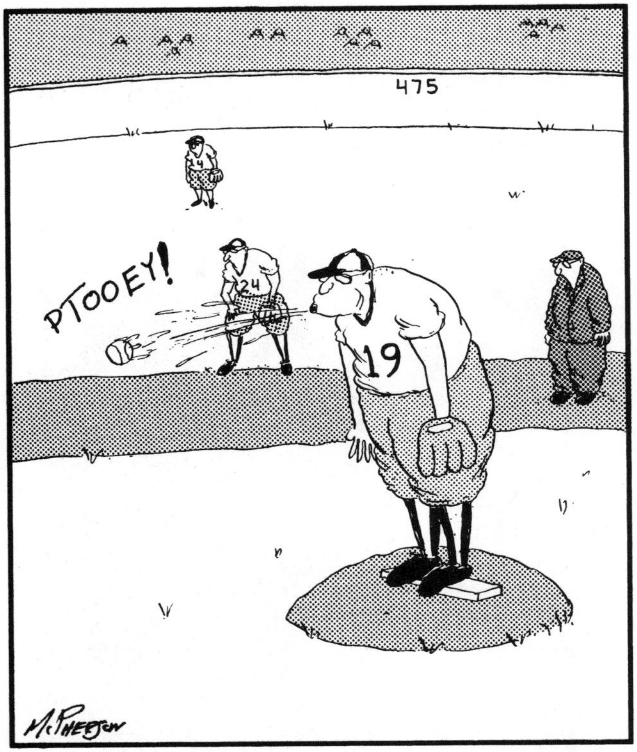
475
PTOOEY!
19
24
McPHERSON

The umpires were starting to suspect that Vern might be throwing a spitball.

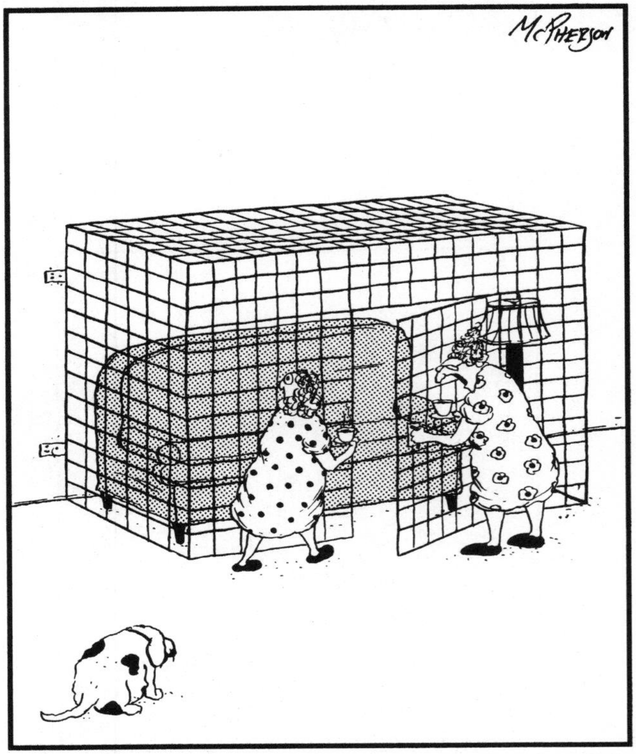
McPHERSON

"And when the dog tracked mud onto the new couch for the third time, it was all Bill could stand."

From the moment Carol's wedding began, guests could tell that it would be no ordinary ceremony.

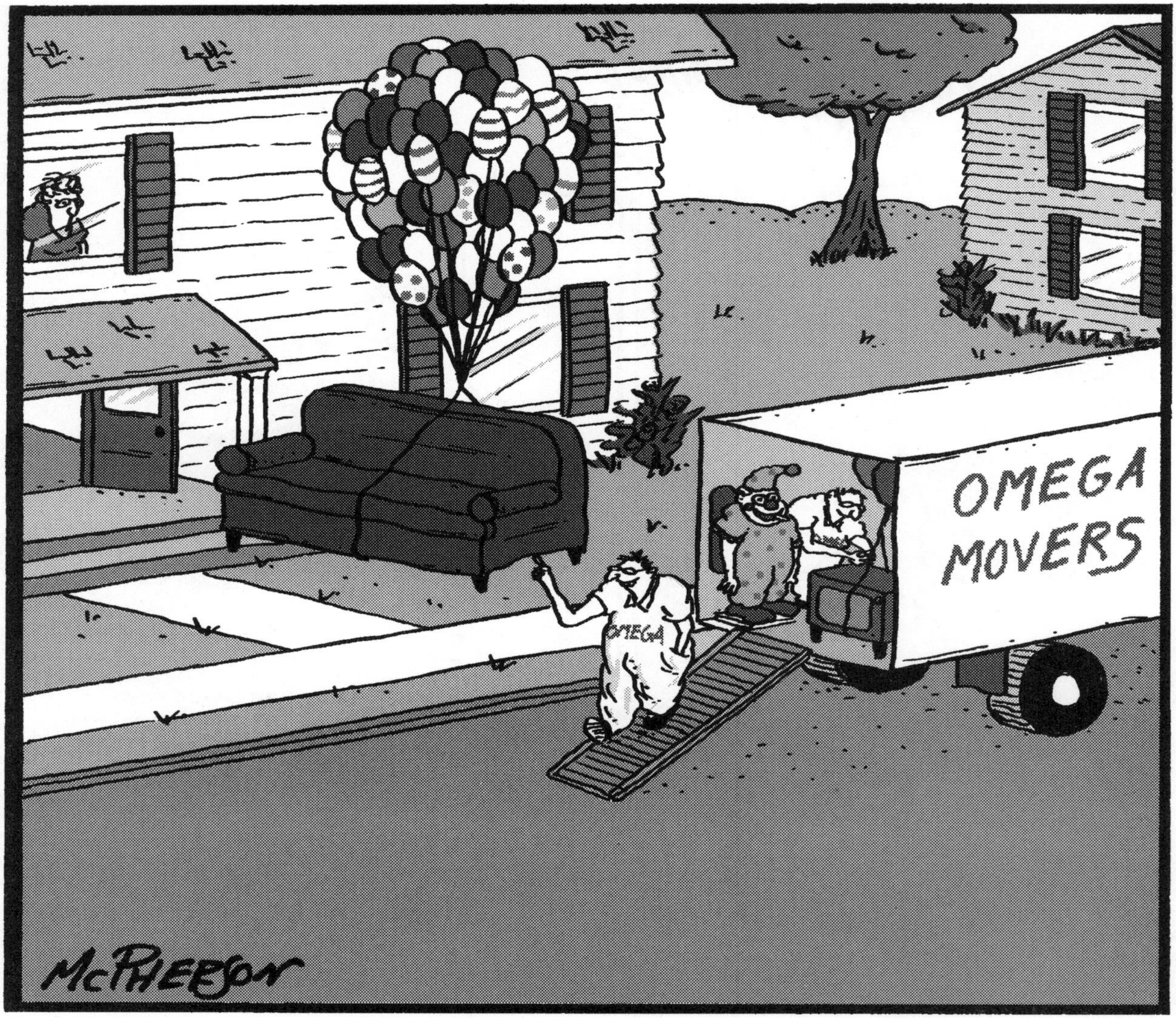
OMEGA
MOVERS
OMEGA
McPHEESON

"This explains the screams we heard coming from the foursome in front of us."

"You should've seen the look on our faces when we realized that we'd been looking at the X-rays backward for the first hour of surgery."

With his identity cleverly concealed, the mysterious neighbor continued to flagrantly walk his dog in other people's yards.

In the midst of final exams, Noreen developed an allergic reaction to algebra.

"There! You see what I mean?! If you catch the light just right, her left tonsil looks exactly like Teddy Roosevelt!"

"Dave! The Hillmans are here and they're going to ask us to help them move! Put on your casts, pronto! And remember, we were in a Rollerblading accident!"

"Mr. Grant! Mr. Marinello! Stop it *right now*,
or no sponge bath for either of you!"

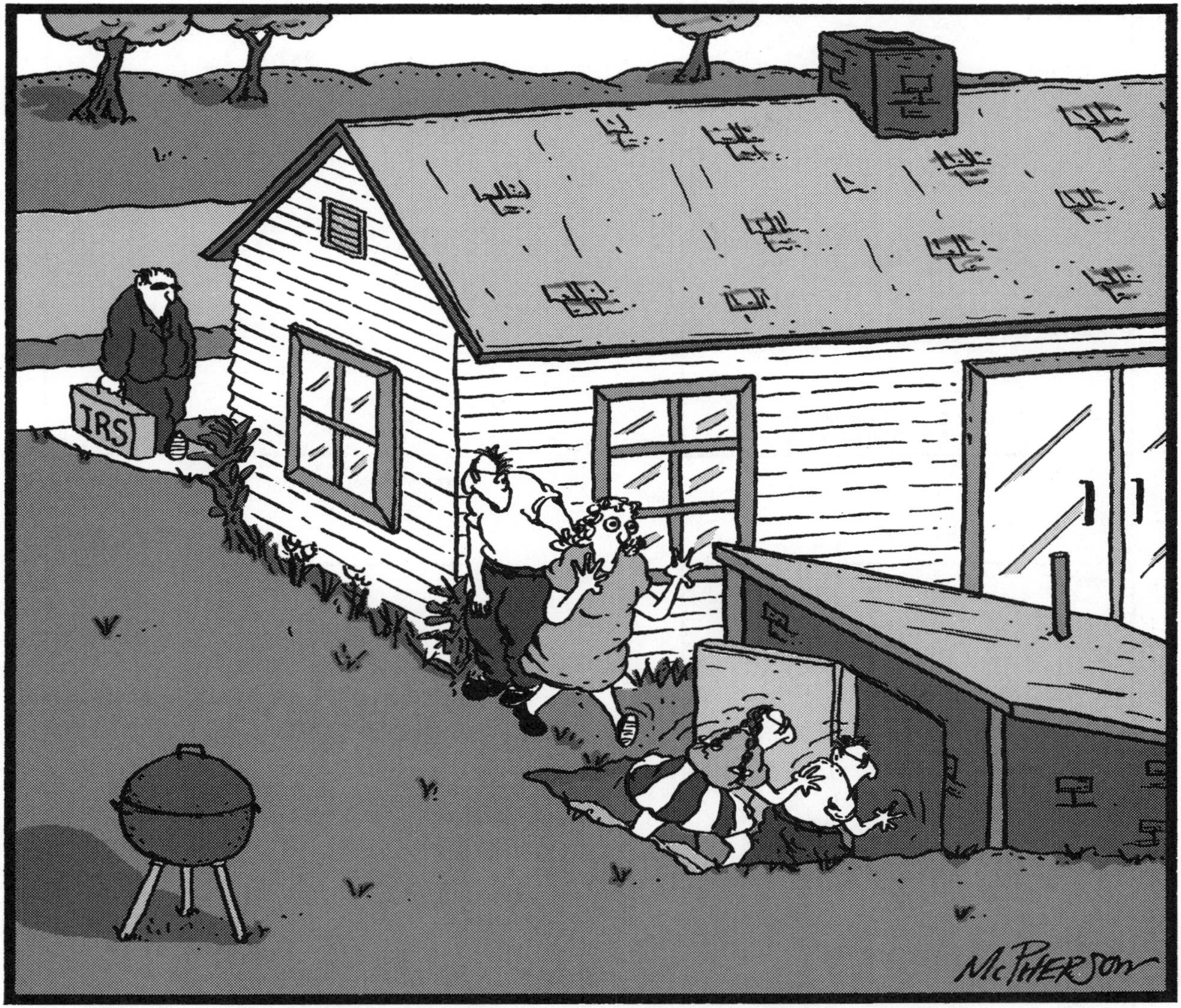
IRS
McPherson

Having spotted the approaching IRS agent, Rodney hurried the family into the tax shelter.

HOW YOU LOOK WHEN YOU'RE SLEEPING.

HOW YOU LOOK TO A MOSQUITO WHEN YOU'RE SLEEPING.

"Which one of you found the fly in your soup?"

"Your HMO allots only one hour to perform hip-replacement surgery. After that, our candy stripers Chip and Brenda will take over."

"That's our new central vacuum system."

24

In an attempt to toughen its graduation standards,
Wilmot High School now required students
to answer one last question
before receiving their diploma.

"And this indicator tells you how many
miles you need to run before you should
attend a high school reunion."

After losing the house to Al in the divorce settlement, Sheila used her gardening skills to carry out one final act of revenge.

Fortunately, an alert waiter spotted Danny's photo on the restaurant's blacklist.

"What rooms would you say the mice have
been most active in, Mrs. Thackler?"

"Only one of them is the real hole. The others
are decoys with Plexiglas covering the holes."

"His parents want to make sure they don't miss seeing him take his first steps."

"Okay, here's the situation. I've got one dose of Novocain left. I can divide it equally among the four of you, or you can draw straws to see who gets it."

"Whoa! Don't hit the horn while people are standing nearby, Mr. Woodward. But trust me: If you get annoyed by slow drivers, this is the car for you."

"Okay, let me get this straight! You gave a door-to-door salesman $300 in cash for this piece of junk, and you never asked for a demonstration?!"

"They're made like that to discourage kids from taking them."

"It's designed specifically for colicky babies."

"It's something the landlord rigged up. If the guy next door snores again tonight, we're supposed to turn that crank nine or ten times really fast."

The Gurnleys interview a new baby sitter.

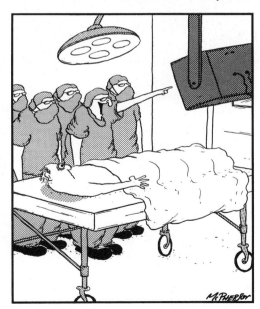

"Stop the tape! See what George Clooney is doing with that catheter? That's the procedure I think we should try with Mr. Simkins."

At last, help for parents who rarely get a chance to talk to each other.

Jerry shows off his new central toilet paper system.

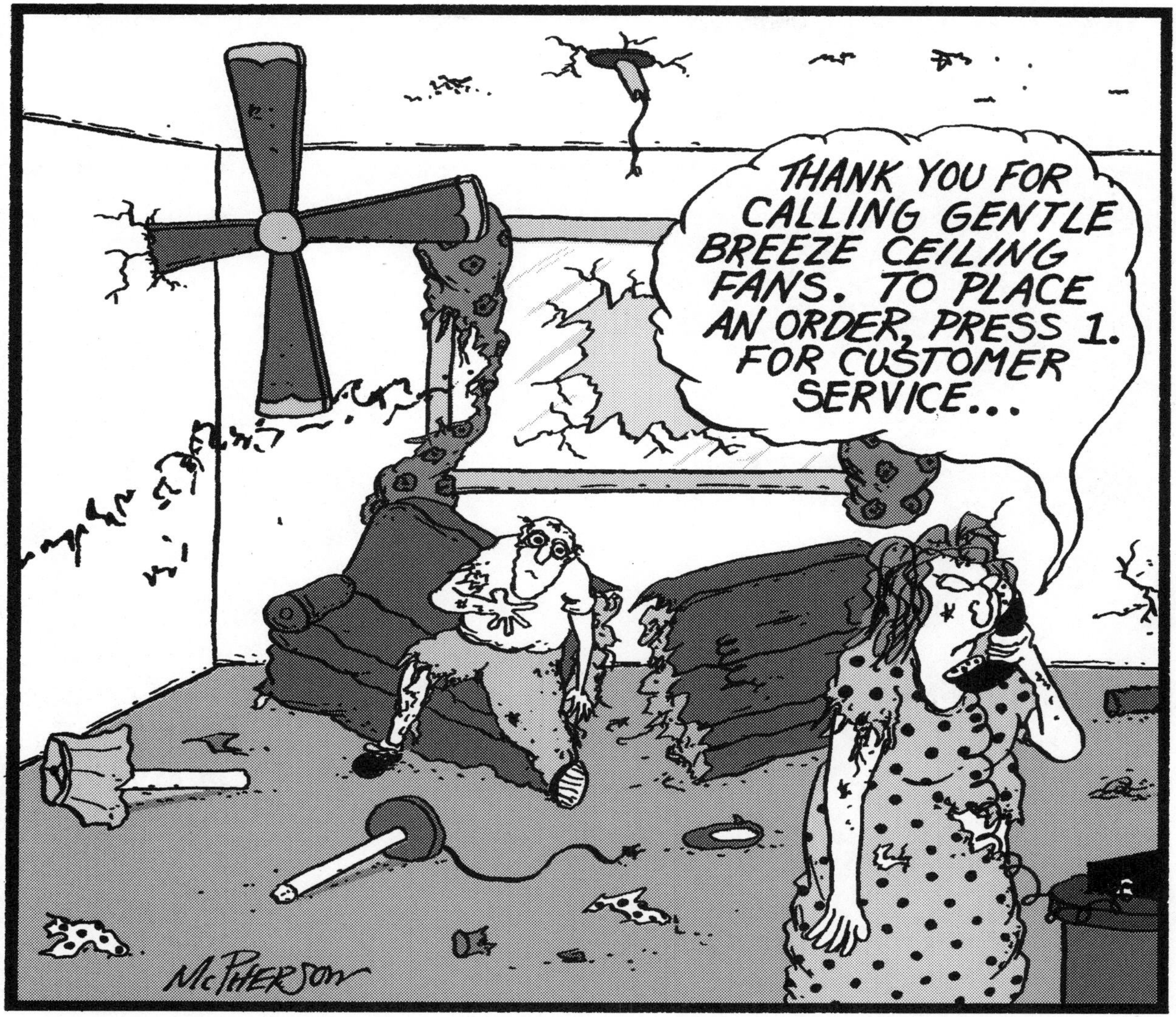
THANK YOU FOR CALLING GENTLE BREEZE CEILING FANS. TO PLACE AN ORDER, PRESS 1. FOR CUSTOMER SERVICE...
McPHERSON

"Unfortunately, I can't find anything in the
PGA rule book that says he can't use it."

"I don't care for that tone of voice!"

"I realize it makes you uneasy, but until you snap out of this sleep-walking phase, Dr. Shadeck says it's for your own good."

"Our fee structure is very simple. We charge a nickel for every ant we kill. Roaches are a quarter."

"It was designed based on research showing the average person burns 500 calories per hour while laughing."

"Well, well, Mr. Seventy-Five in a forty-five mile-per-hour zone! You really had me going until I noticed the trapdoor under the steering column!"

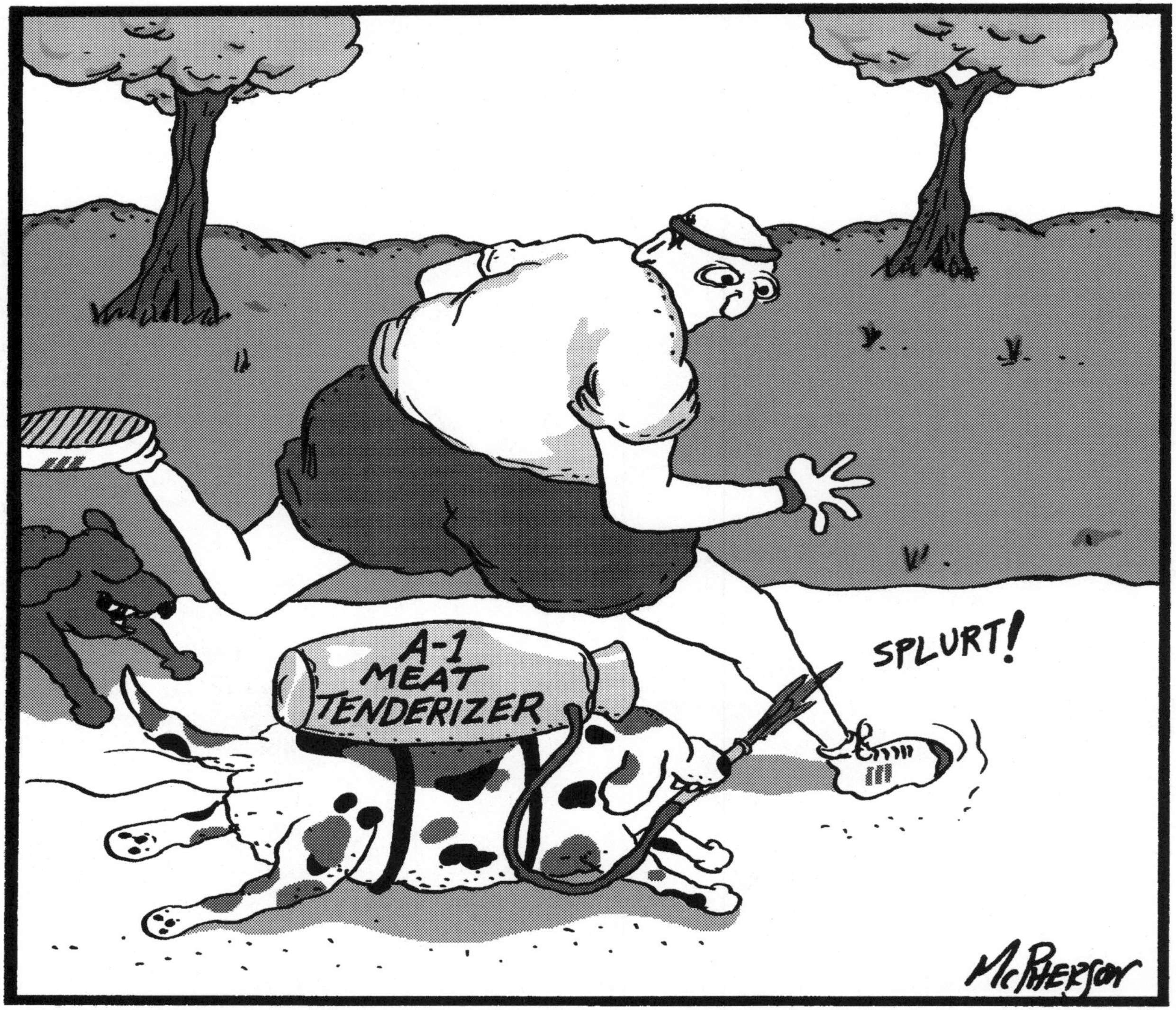
A-1
MEAT
TENDERIZER
SPLURT!
McPHERSON

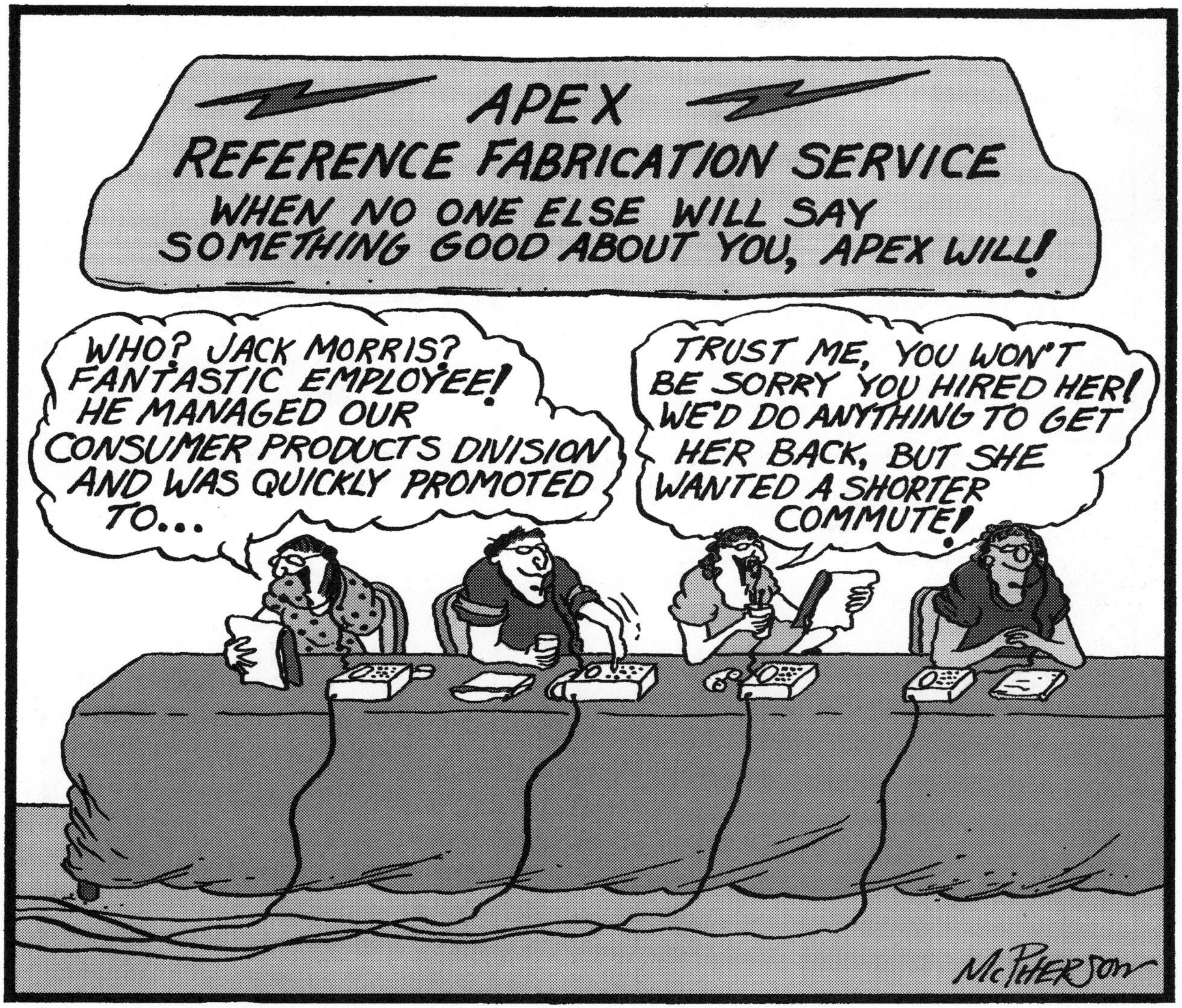
APEX
REFERENCE FABRICATION SERVICE
WHEN NO ONE ELSE WILL SAY SOMETHING GOOD ABOUT YOU, APEX WILL!
WHO? JACK MORRIS? FANTASTIC EMPLOYEE! HE MANAGED OUR CONSUMER PRODUCTS DIVISION AND WAS QUICKLY PROMOTED TO...
TRUST ME, YOU WON'T BE SORRY YOU HIRED HER! WE'D DO ANYTHING TO GET HER BACK, BUT SHE WANTED A SHORTER COMMUTE!
McPHERSON

"Bill can't bear the thought of killing a mouse, so he rigged a way to fling them into the neighbor's yard."

"For Pete's sake, slow down! This is that stretch where there's always a speed trap!"

"Whoa! Don't help him, Mike. According to this note, he burped, causing another golfer in his foursome to miss a two-foot eagle putt."

Waitress Clarice Fullman was rapidly approaching job burnout.

"For heaven's sake, Alan! Get the skimmer!"

"These new Holly Heimlich dolls are the hottest thing since the Cabbage Patch Kids."

"That's the third time she's solved it in the last twenty minutes."

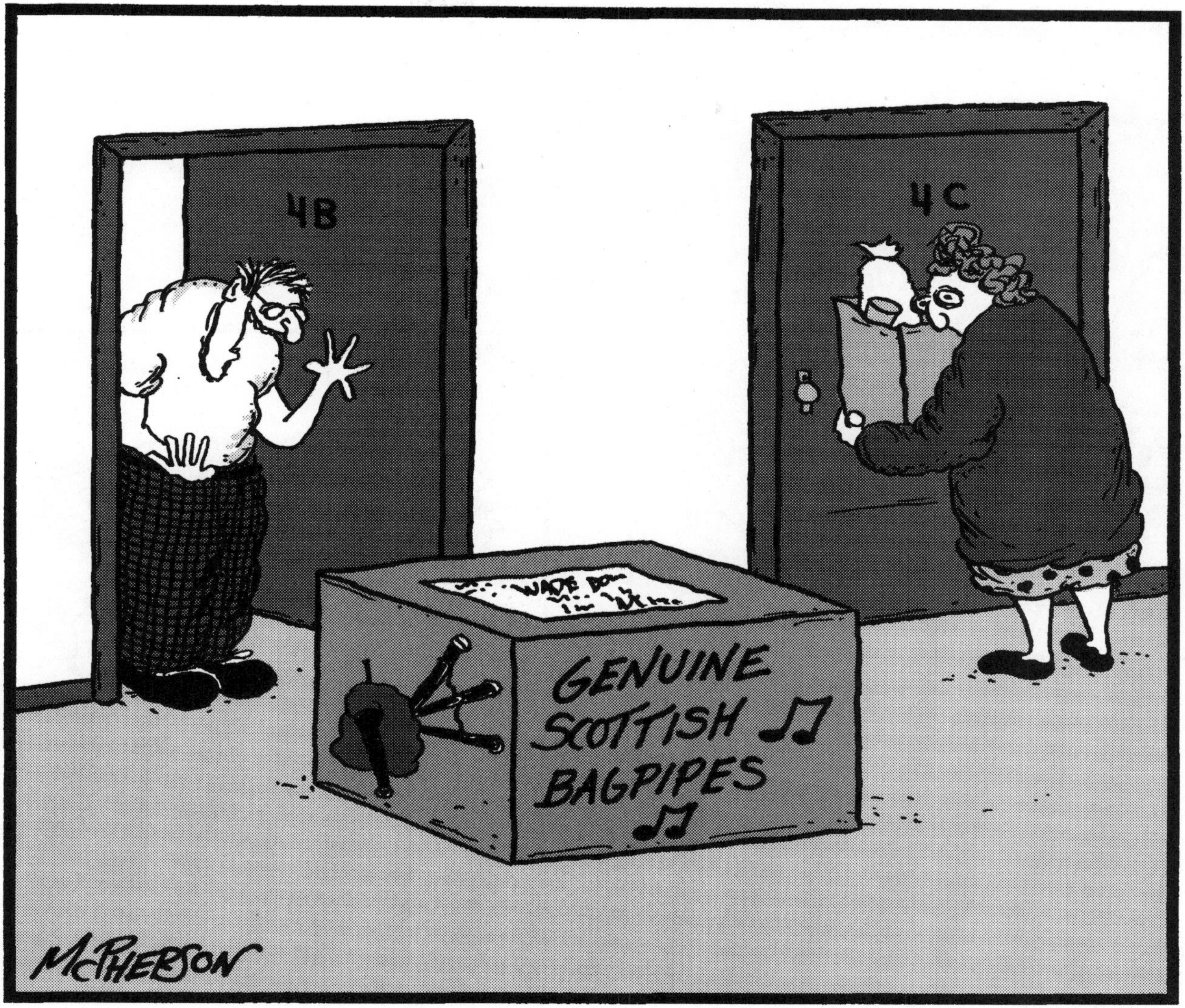
4B
4C
GENUINE
SCOTTISH
BAGPIPES
McPHERSON

"Good heavens! I don't know whether we're
incredibly fortunate or incredibly *unfortunate*!"

"Not only will I *never* baby-sit for you again, it's
gonna cost you a hundred bucks to keep me from
squealing to the other sitters about your kids!"

"For me it started out as a horrendous sinus infection, followed by an intense earache and crippling stomach pains. Now all I've got is a hacking cough and this uncontrollable drooling."

"For twenty dollars I can get rid of that mole on your nose after I'm done filling this cavity."

"This vehicle doesn't have four-wheel drive, but if you ever get stuck somewhere, all you need to do is light that fuse over there."

"The kitty-litter truck is here."

Boyd Wincott tackles one of Pinemont Country Club's infamous Jell-O traps.

"The doctor says it's just a pinched nerve."

"Looks like you're the victim of the latest fad in vandalism. Somebody took out your sunroof and put a big magnifying glass in its place."

With the help of acupuncture, Gary was able to trim eleven strokes off his game.

"Believe me, we tried everything to soothe her colic. Car rides, massage, yoga, mud baths. Then one day, out of desperation . . ."

"We like to try all our options before using drugs to induce labor."

"Oh, thank heavens! It was just you! I thought a meteor hit the roof!"

"I think I can fix that chair."

"Unfortunately, the video you're renting was not rewound by the previous renters. However, here's their home address along with a complimentary bag of rotten tomatoes."

"Go ahead and tee off. Then I want you
to listen to this wheezing."

"I don't expect any problems, but
just to be on the safe side, I'd like to give you
a shot of Novocain in each ear."

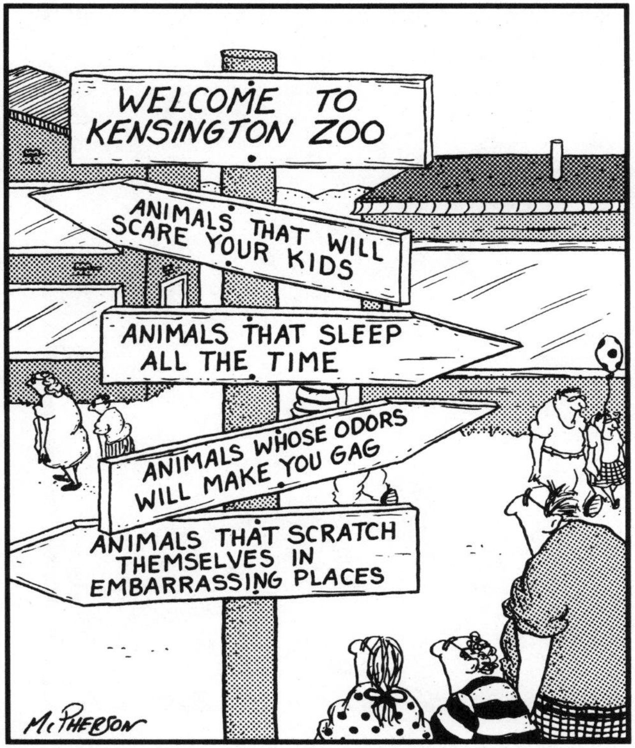
WELCOME TO KENSINGTON ZOO
ANIMALS THAT WILL SCARE YOUR KIDS
ANIMALS THAT SLEEP ALL THE TIME
ANIMALS WHOSE ODORS WILL MAKE YOU GAG
ANIMALS THAT SCRATCH THEMSELVES IN EMBARRASSING PLACES
McPHERSON

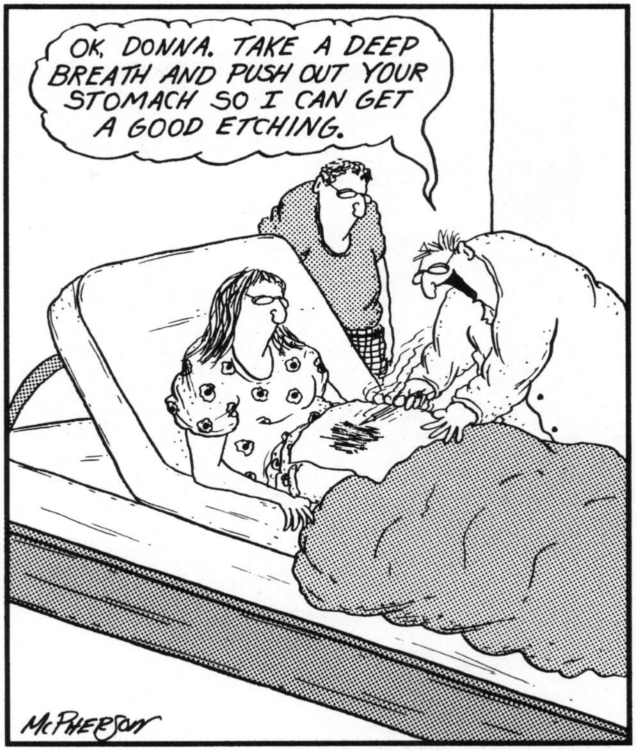
OK, DONNA. TAKE A DEEP BREATH AND PUSH OUT YOUR STOMACH SO I CAN GET A GOOD ETCHING.
McPHERSON

Budget ultrasound.

**From that moment on, Ed was referred to
by all who knew him as "Big Foot."**

For one fleeting instant, while all the other adults weren't looking, Dave watched dumbstruck as every baby in the maternity ward did the Wave.

"If you ask me, the staff here gets a little too attached to the lobsters."

"Ooh! Ooh! I just saw one!! He stuck his little gray mousey nose out from under the couch, and then he . . . he scooted over toward the lamp!"

Glenda was a master of turning adversity into opportunity.

"Your insurance company is refusing to pay your medical bills due to a pre-existing condition. It says you were already an idiot before you decided to Rollerblade down the interstate."

"Yep, it's yours, all right! Top Flite three!
Tough break hombre!"

"I think I hit a stone."

PLINK!

"Now, now sweetie. That was an *outdoor* voice. We need to remember to use our *indoor* voices when we're inside."

"I don't *care* if there's a special on Junior Mints! Just tell me what aisle the hornet spray is in!"

"It's called the B-chip! It installs discreetly on the back of your TV and prevents anyone in your family from watching 'Baywatch.'"

The scourge of vinyl car seats.

The latest trend in baby sitting: surcharges.

"I calculated that by the year 2012, we will have spent $78,760 for their allowances."

"Well, it figures! We're seven-tenths of a mile
past the warranty!"

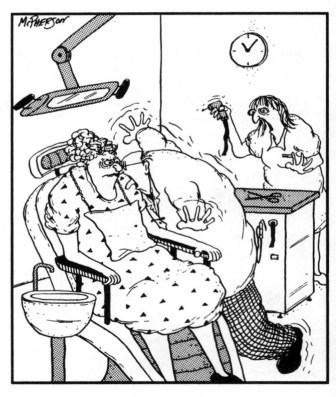

"Okay, Mrs. Claver! There, see?! I cut the
line to the drill! No drilling today!
Now, let go of Dr. Selman's nose!"

"Will you relax?! No one is going to see you wearing my dress!"

A demanding final phase is added to the National Medical Boards.

"Well, cleaning the litter boxes just got a whole lot easier! Check out this new vacuum attachment!"

"No, this mixture is no good. That rat turned green and lost most of its fur. Let's go with thirty milligrams of Xylonene. That should be fine for Mrs. Turner."

Seventy-two percent of all infants carry the anti-car seat gene, allowing their stiffened bodies to resist forces in excess of 100 pounds per square inch.

"Trust me, this is the best way to learn."

"Our special tonight is fifteen seconds at our pasta buffet for $3.95, or for those of you who are watching your weight, seven seconds for $2.95."

"Before you try on any bathing suit, you're required to sign this waiver releasing us from liability should you incur permanent damage to your self-esteem."

"Here's twenty bucks. Make sure that the plaid chair never gets there."

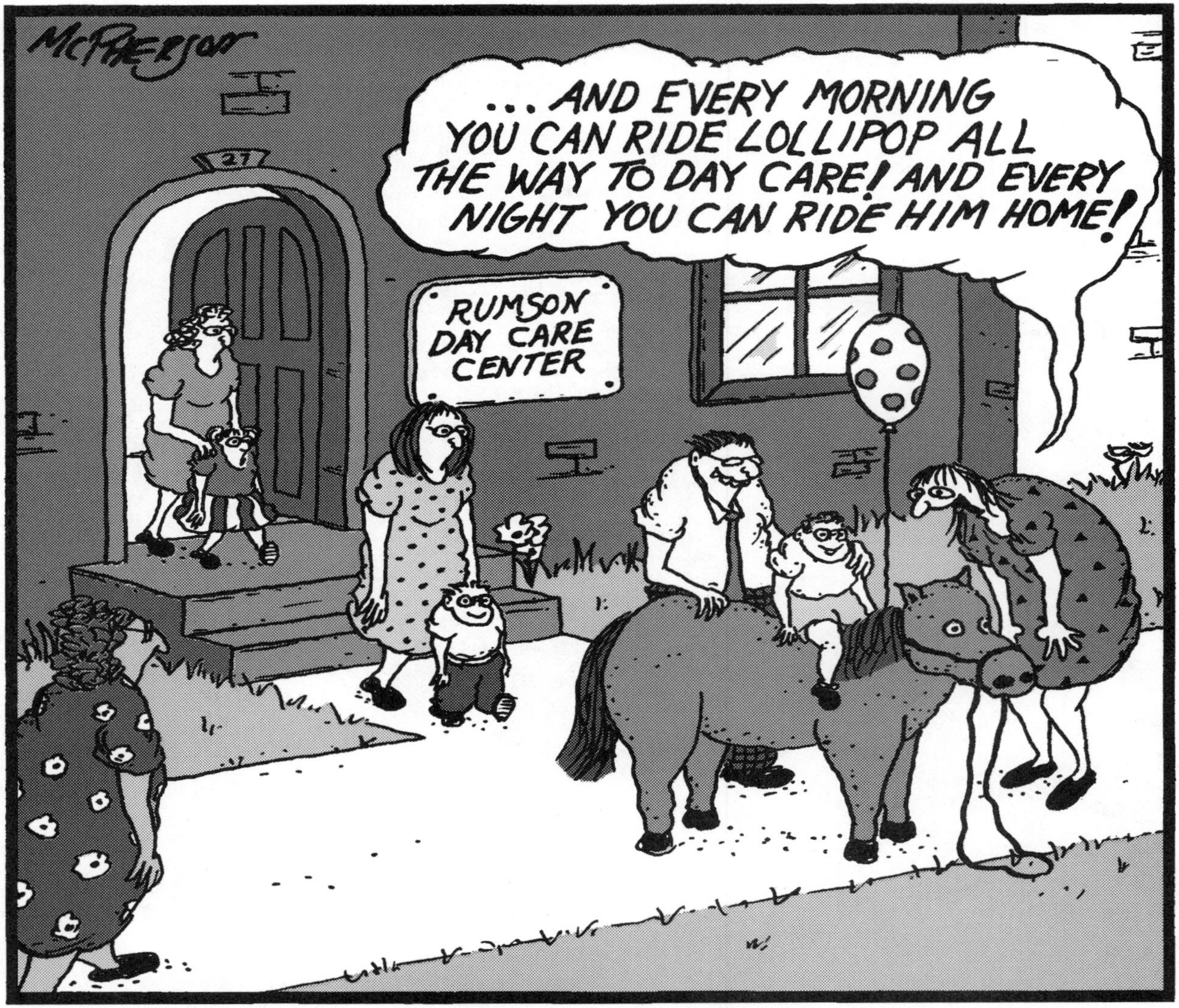
MCPHERSON
27
...AND EVERY MORNING YOU CAN RIDE LOLLIPOP ALL THE WAY TO DAY CARE! AND EVERY NIGHT YOU CAN RIDE HIM HOME!
RUMSON DAY CARE CENTER

Day-care guilt.

"I'm sorry, Mr. Credley, but due to our new truth-in-advertising policy, your request for a vanity plate reading 'BUFF-HUNK' has been denied."

Thanks to her Early Tantrum Warning Device, Cathy had ninety seconds to take evasive action.

"Will you two knock it off with the train sound effects?!"

DECEMBER 17, 1989

"That's the high-water mark from Dan's little foray into plumbing."

"Sorry to have to redo this, but Carol Ann
is pretty sure that her missing earring
is in here somewhere."

"If there are any among us who know of some
reason why Dave and Lynette should not be
joined together, let them speak now or forever . . ."

75

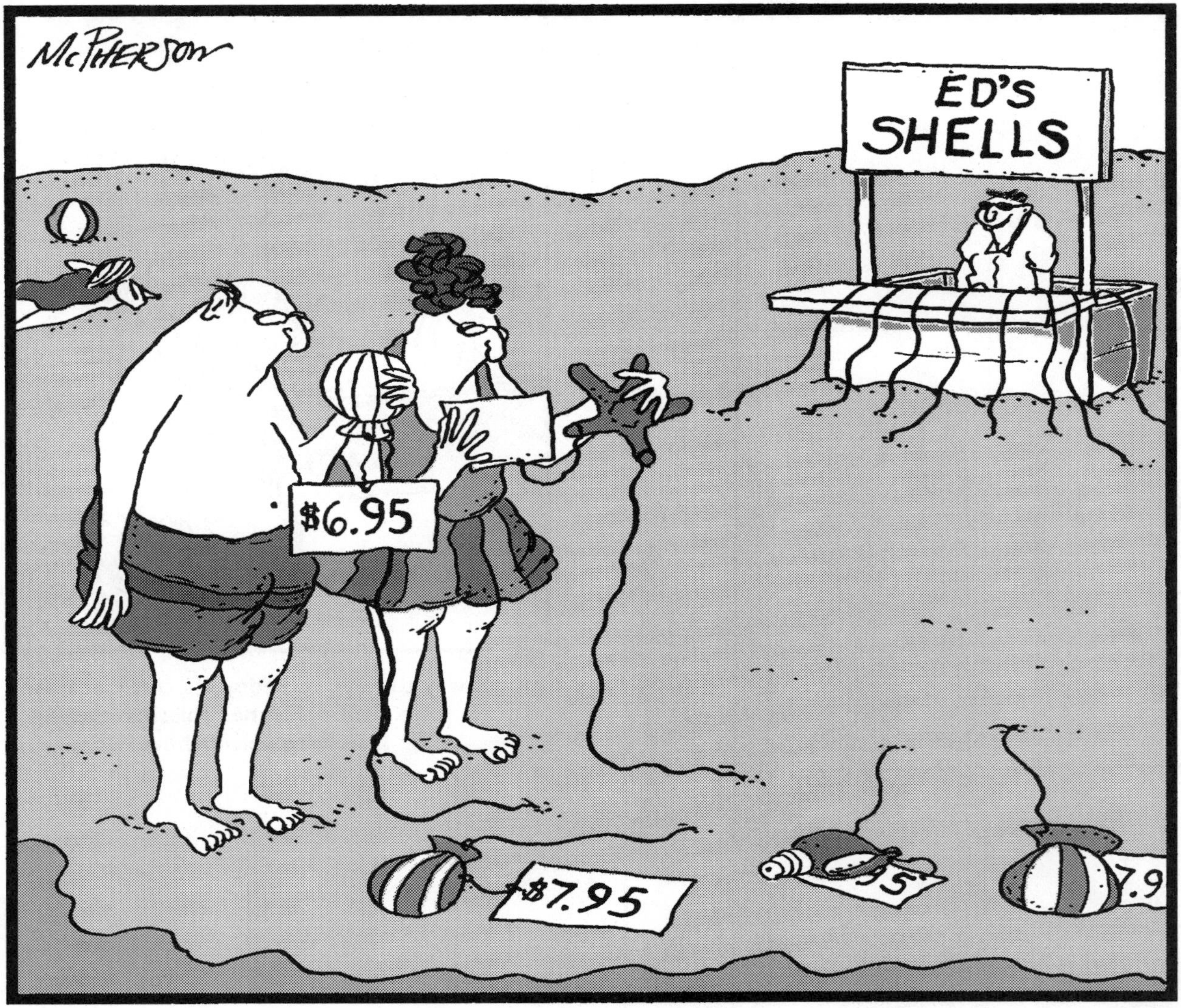
McPHERSON
ED'S SHELLS
$6.95
$7.95

Disaster strikes the county fair.

"They're made like that to keep people from drinking straight out of the container."

"For an extra twenty-five dollars, Ruth here will crouch behind you and tug on the back of your scalp so it'll look like you've had a facelift."

"Okay, hang on! I'm gonna slam on the brakes so the bee will smack against the windshield!"

"Jason! You apologize to Mr. Feffler this instant! Or no pudding for you tonight, young man!"

"Now *that*, Mr. Fillman, is what I call an ingrown toenail!"

"I'm sorry, miss, but a Polaroid of you blowing out twenty-one candles on a birthday cake doesn't qualify as a photo I.D."

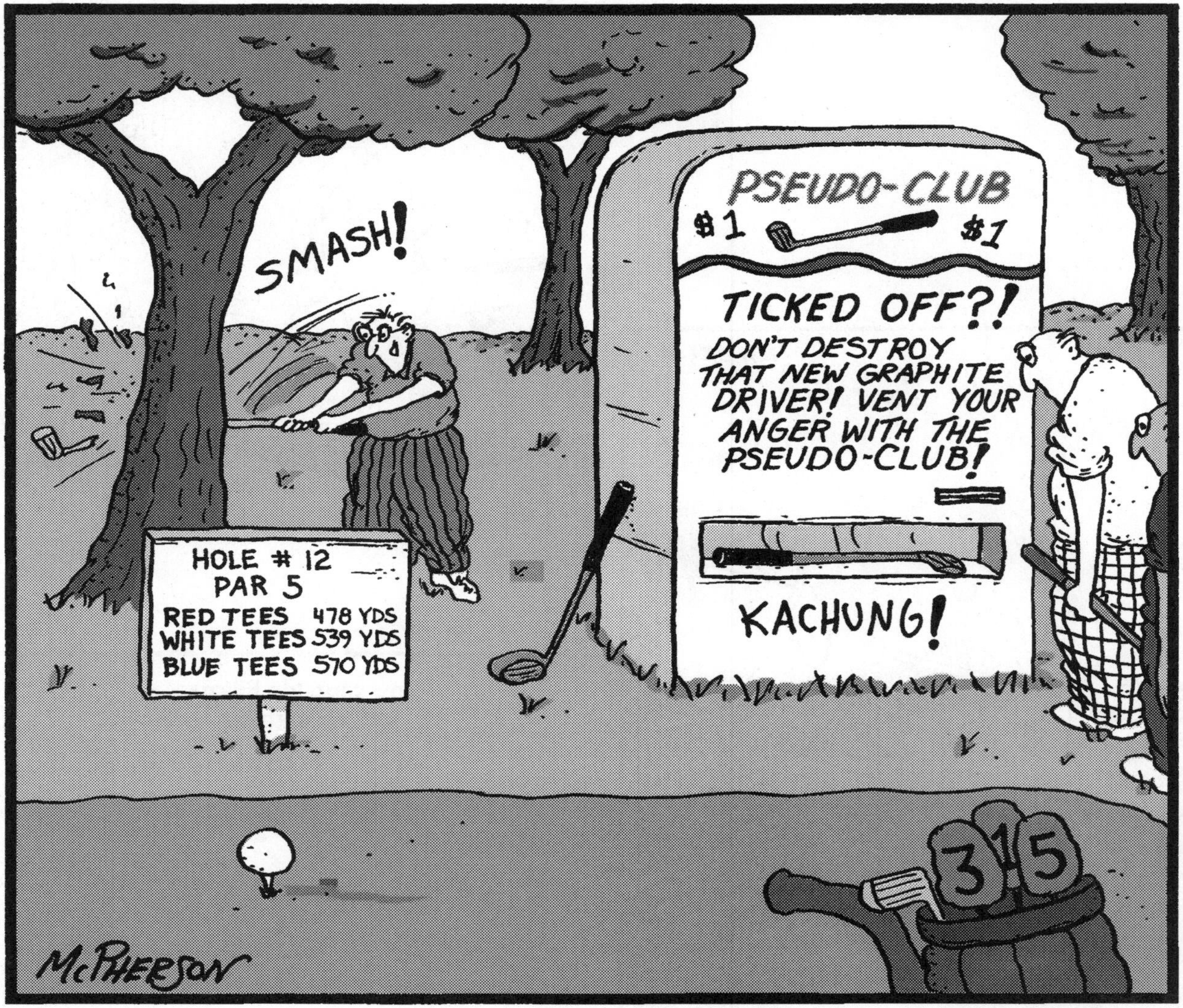
SMASH!
PSEUDO-CLUB
$1 $1
TICKED OFF?!
DON'T DESTROY THAT NEW GRAPHITE DRIVER! VENT YOUR ANGER WITH THE PSEUDO-CLUB!
KACHUNG!
HOLE # 12
PAR 5
RED TEES 478 YDS
WHITE TEES 539 YDS
BLUE TEES 570 YDS
3 1 5
McPHERSON

"Gary here will try to infiltrate their operation to see if he can locate their nest."

"Well, good news! Your mortgage has been approved! However, we require that from now on you get written permission from us to make any purchases over fifty dollars."

Bill lets Brenda know that while he appreciates her help, he would prefer that she keep her insightful comments to herself.

"Notice Roy's flawless body language here,
shaking his head from side to side
while letting out one long, steady whistle."

"The only frames that are covered by your
insurance are the two on the top row.
Any of the others will be an additional $150."

"Well, there are only two seats left.
I can put you next to a three-year-old with an
ear infection, or a seventy-five-year-old
who will spend the entire flight telling you
about his recent prostate surgery."

"If either of you bite into what seems to be an
almond slice, don't eat it. I broke off a nail
while I was scooping your cones."

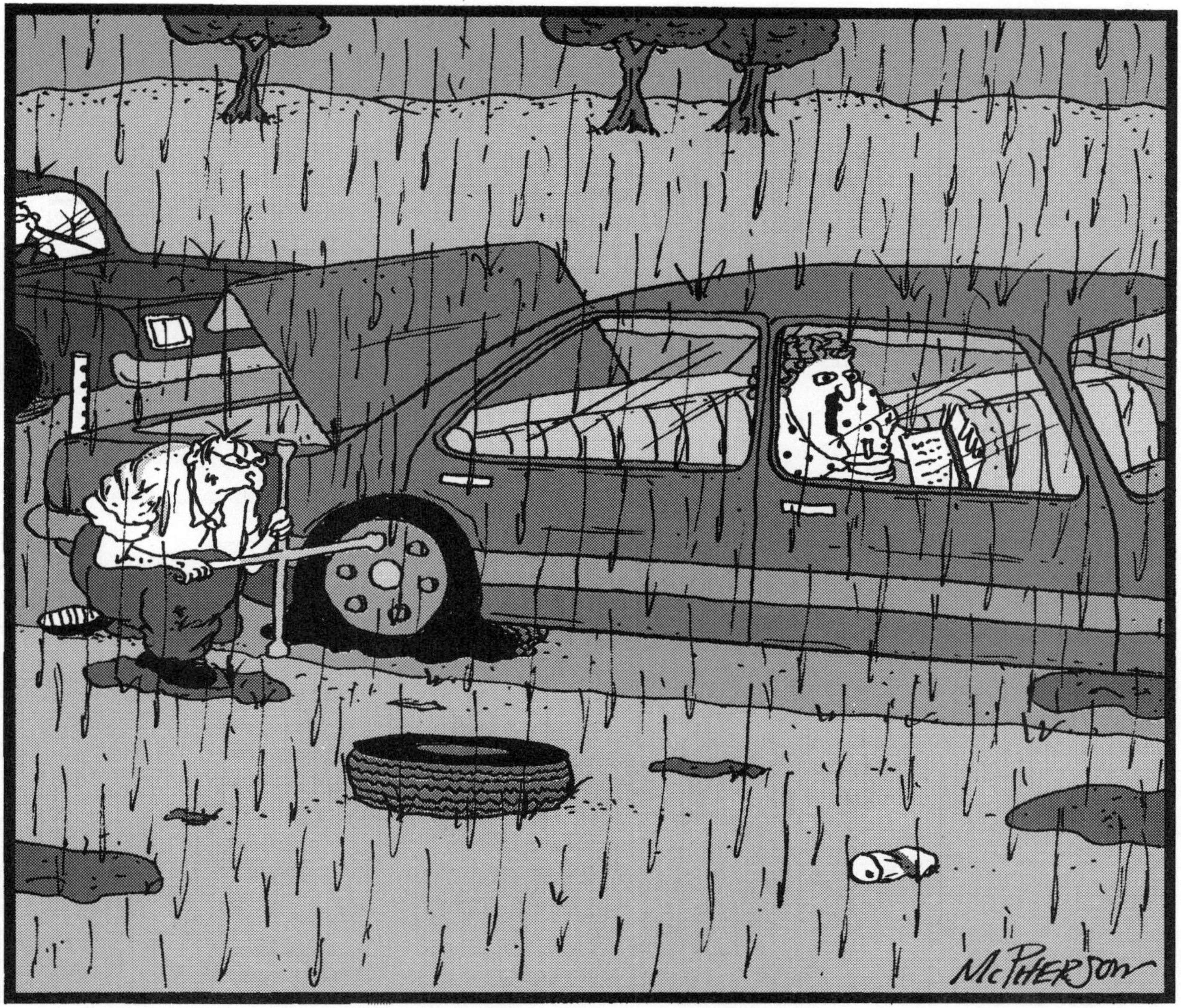
McPHERSON

"Ray! There's a bug in here!"

"A winning lottery ticket? Gosh, I sure think we'd remember if we found something like that! Ha, ha!"

"I *told* you not to pick at it!"

"Distressed furniture is very popular these days."

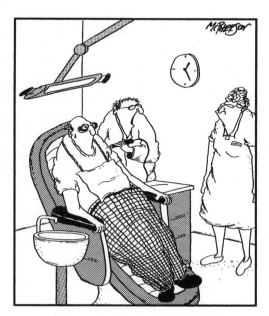

"Cleona, do me a favor and take the
batteries out of the smoke detector.
I'm going to do some serious drilling here."

"I'll give you a hundred bucks if you'll watch my
kids for twenty minutes while I take a nap."

"Our driving examiner is out sick, so you'll be taking your road test here. You need to score 900 points to get your license."

"Sorry it smells like gasoline. I put it on top of the engine so it would stay warm for you."

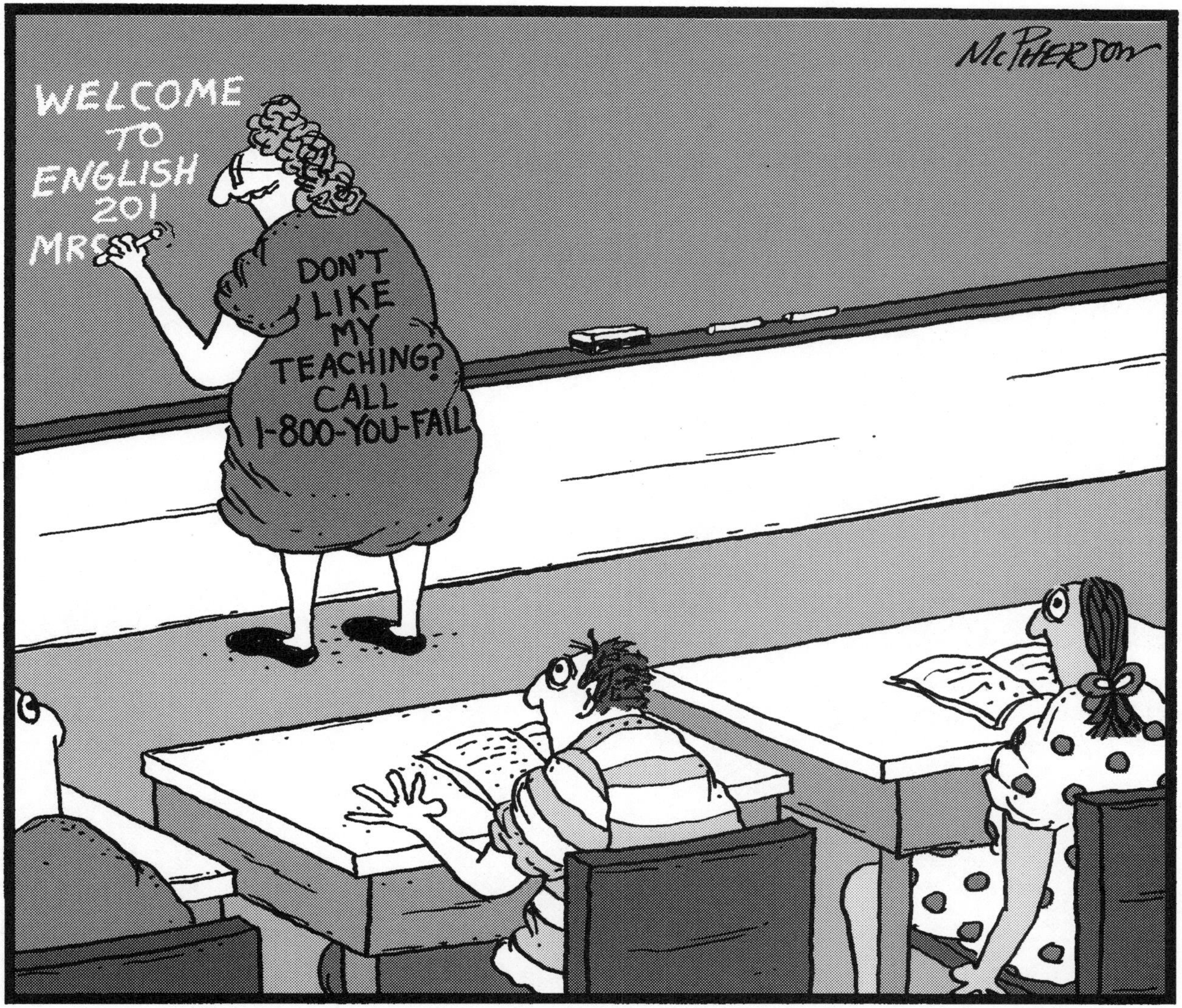
McPHERSON
WELCOME TO ENGLISH 201 MRS
DON'T LIKE MY TEACHING? CALL 1-800-YOU-FAIL

Every now and then, Dr. Walston liked to put up his joke eye chart.

Through the addition of free weights, a once-popular fad becomes the latest fitness craze.

"Just stay submerged and keep calm, ma'am. Ray here found a piece of your suit, and other staff members are looking for the rest."

"I'm sorry, sir, but your insurance company requires that you first get a referral slip from your primary care physician before we can treat you."

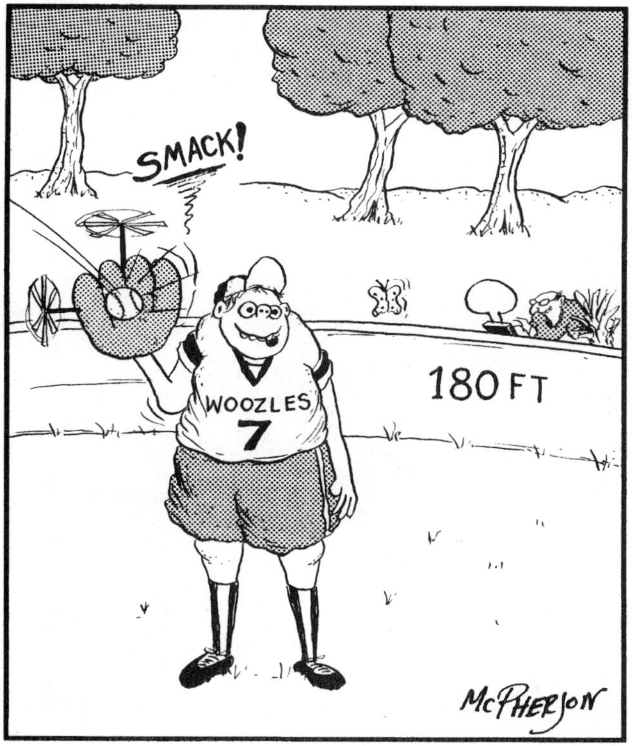
SMACK!
WOOZLES
7
180 FT
McPHERSON

Little League officials soon got wise to Jason's dad and the remote-control glove.

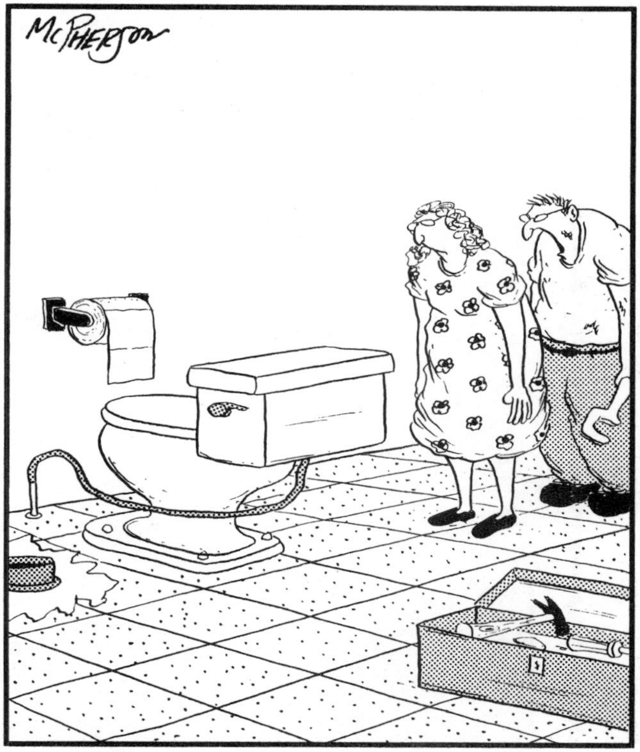
McPHERSON

"Okay, there! I don't want to hear any more whining about how hard it is to reach the toilet paper!"

Using technology to allay your child's fears.

By 2003, Congress will require that all new cars be designed to emit a stream of red smoke anytime they exceed sixty-five miles per hour.

"Apparently you folks haven't quite grasped
the concept of our No-dicker-sticker-pricing.
Let's go over it one more time."

"For the love of Pete! Will you just
return their stupid lawn mower?!"

"Will you quit whimpering! They're not carnivores!"

Always a practical joker, Carl tosses an old rib bone
onto the floor at the height of his
chiropractic session.

Using stimulus/response, the Nelsons hoped to discourage Jeremy from engaging in dangerous activities as a teenager.

"Here, I rigged this up to help with your poison ivy."

"Having completely covered any areas of the room that are not to be painted, light the four cherry bombs and throw them into the paint distribution pan. Leave the room immediately."

"They made me leave my shirt and pants as collateral
until we return the gas can."

"The owner of the amusement park called and said he'll give us free passes for next year if we don't say a word about this to the press."

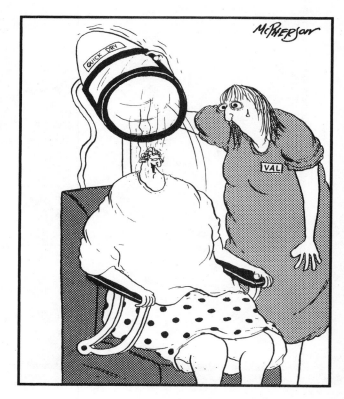

"Wooo! Thank heavens! I was starting to think you'd forgotten about me!"

"These should clear up the condition in about ten days. However, if you notice the slightest sign that you're growing an udder, call your doctor immediately."

An essential parenting skill: speeding up bedtime by condensing children's books.

Wanting simply to face the inevitable, many parents have begun to organize chicken pox parties.

"I admire your interest in natural childbirth, but you've gotta be glad we talked you into having that epidural!"

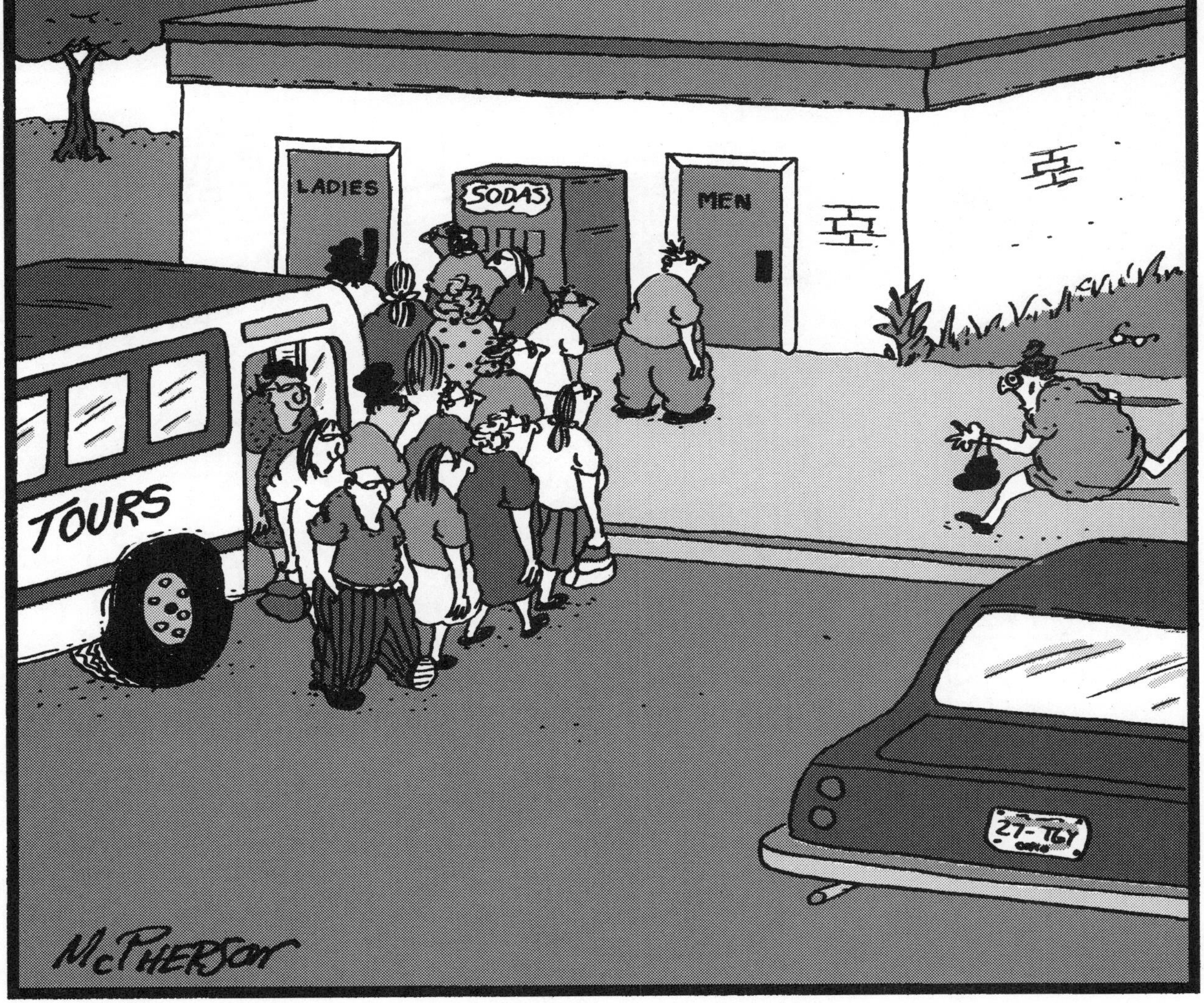
LADIES
SODAS
MEN
TOURS
27-T6Y
McPHERSON

"Hey, wait a minute! Aren't you the woman who runs the
Happy Tush Diaper Service?!"

"I'm sorry, Mrs. Morris, but to prevent office visits from dragging on, the HMO requires that I answer only 'yes' or 'no' questions."

"Refresh our memory. What was the problem with your car?"

"Beautiful! Now all we need to do is sit back and wait for that jerk downstairs to crank up his stereo!"

"Oh, one more thing. If Gregory starts to show any signs that he might throw a tantrum, lock yourself inside the cage, put on the helmet, and call 911 immediately."

To soften their public image, many states have introduced singing troopers.

"If you ask me, the paperboy is getting brash."

"Now *that* was one serious skid mark!"

"It's the latest thing in home security systems. Makes your house look like a dump so no one will even *think* about breaking in."

"These are the ultrasound technicians
who incorrectly told you you'd be having a girl.
Grace has offered to re-wallpaper your nursery
and Brenda will return any gender-specific gifts
that you received."

"Oh, wow! It's a birth announcement from the Fulkersons! They just had twin boys!"

Dave hadn't lost a ball in seven years.

Prospective dates first had to give a
full presentation to Debbie Wexler's parents.

"The humor section? Uh, sure.
Third aisle on the left, near the magazines."

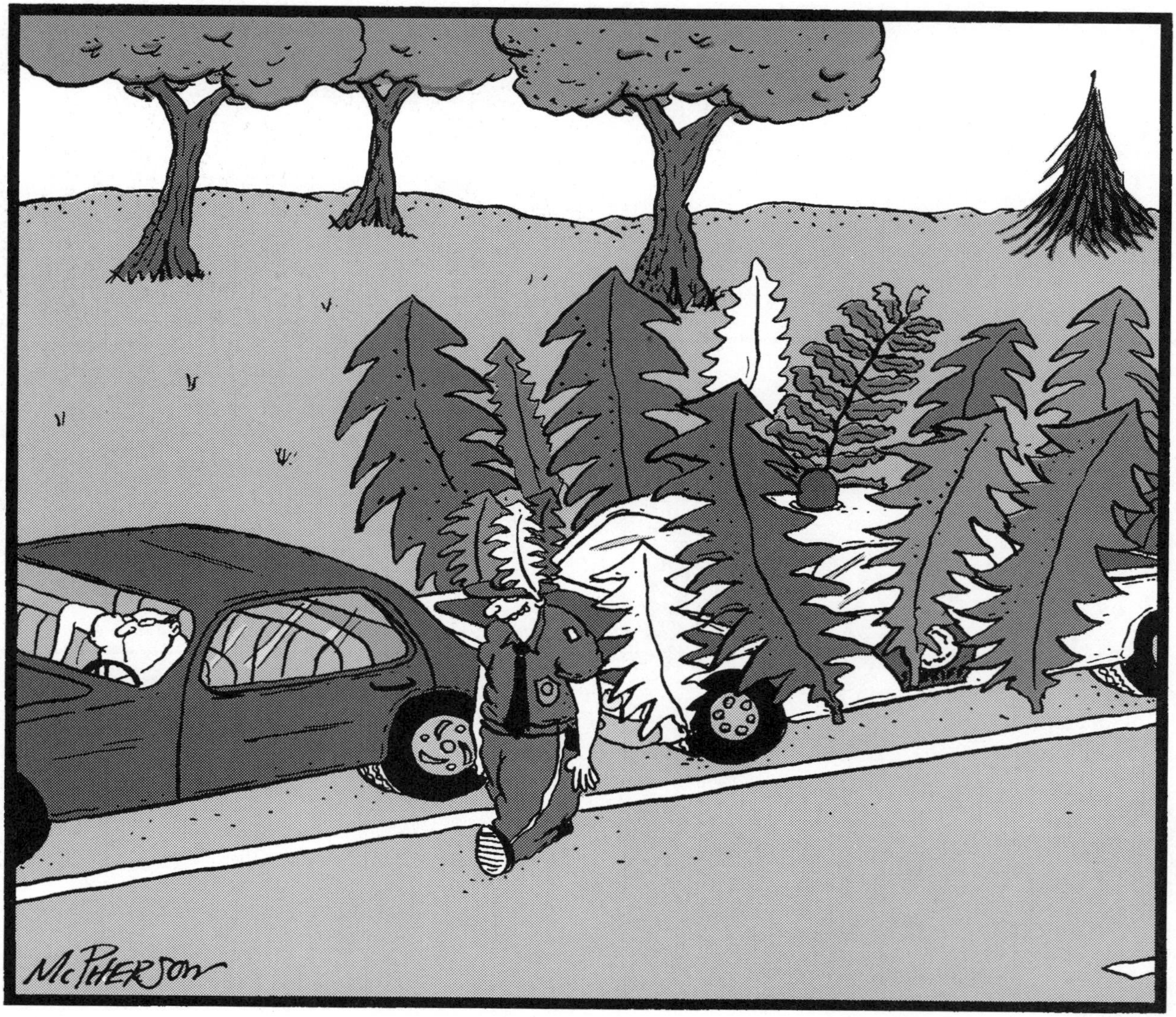
McPHERSON

"Okay, let's see . . . Mr. Philmont and Tippy."

Carol makes a last-ditch effort to
keep the kids from missing the bus.

How we get on junk mail lists.

After getting a good look at her date as he came
up the walk, Diane gives the signal to her mom.

Randy awakens in the midst of another
of his flying dreams.

"I know that many of you are squeamish about dissecting a frog, so as an incentive, three of the frogs have been implanted with concert tickets to Smashing Pumpkins."

"Check out this goofball! Is he a candidate for the Dufus Hall of Fame or what?! Make a copy of this for the scrapbook."

Ted scores the parking spot of his career.

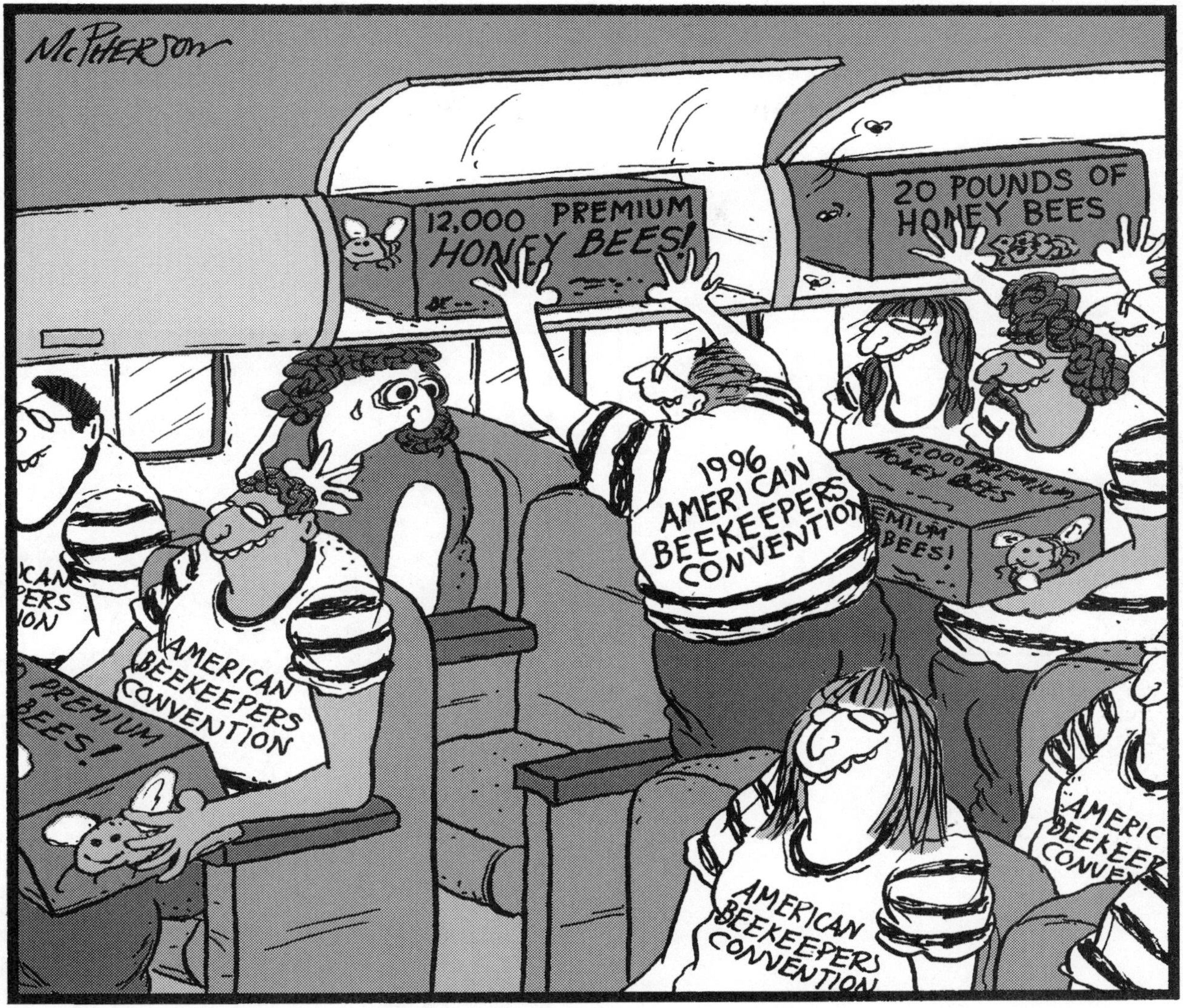
McPHERSON
12,000 PREMIUM HONEY BEES!
20 POUNDS OF HONEY BEES
1996 AMERICAN BEEKEEPERS CONVENTION
AMERICAN BEEKEEPERS CONVENTION
AMERICAN BEEKEEPERS CONVENTION

"How much did you want? Half a pound?"

Striving to avoid a tuition hike, Dawson University looked for other ways to generate revenue.

In every office there is always one person who consistently microwaves disgusting-smelling food.

"I tell you we love it. You just pop off the tabletop
and slide the whole thing into the dishwasher."

"Dr. Nilsteen, calm down! Take a deep breath. You *know* you can do this!
Those incidents last week with Mr. Maxwell and Mrs. Hudak
were just freak accidents."

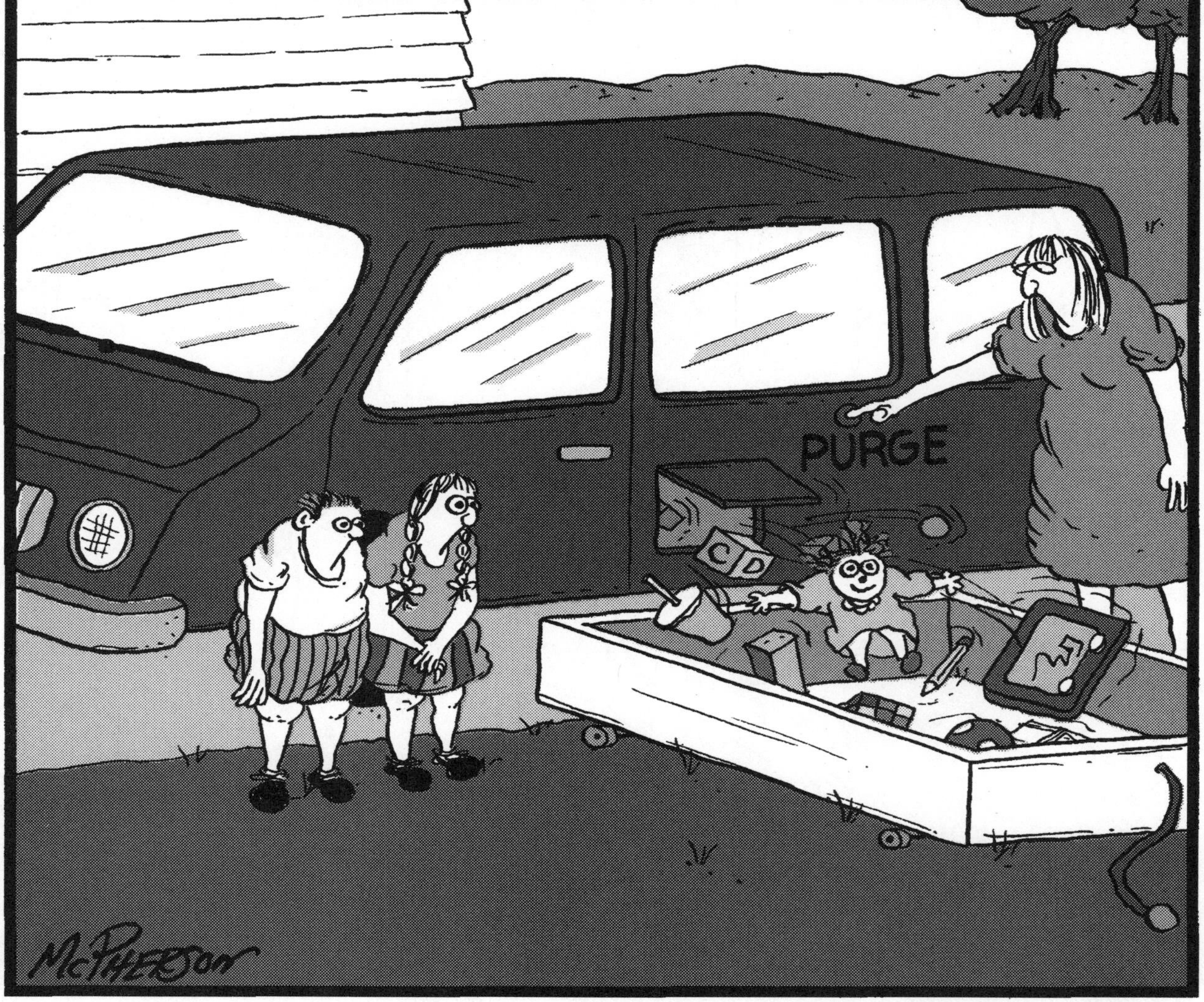
PURGE
McPHERSON

More and more couples are installing
morning-breath exhaust hoods.

Much to Larry's dismay, Brooke renews her
membership to the Cat-of-the-Month Club.

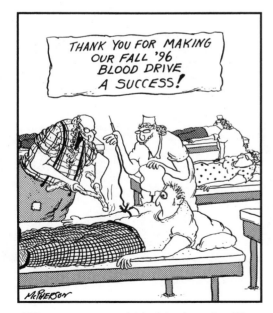

"I'd say you want to stick it right about there! Yep,
there's a real gusher right where that mole is!"

The final hurdle for becoming vested in
the company's pension plan: running the
managers' wet-towel gauntlet.

Lyle's ability to tie flies to Linda Sandusky's hair earned him twenty-seven weeks of detention study hall.

"Ma'am, there are others waiting."

"Whoa! Come on, Lois! That gap is *way* too narrow!
You know the rule: six inches, *minimum*."

"... and when it's time for you to buy new sneakers,
the *least* expensive pair will be the ones you want.
Any other pair will seem laughable by comparison ..."

How most college students decide on a major.

One of the many new screened-in, bug-free communities.

After exhausting days and long commutes from their respective offices, Bob and Kay give each other the look that says: "I thought *you* were going to pick up the kids from day care!"

"Well, I'm no psychic, but I sense some frustration with piano lessons."

"Look, why don't we save ourselves a lot of time and trouble. You give us all of your candy, turn out your lights and go to bed, and we'll be honor-bound not to go to any other homes."

"Dust, cotton, wood, insects, plastic, wallpaper, and socks."

"Thirty-seven! How many have you found?"

The latest in specialty parenting magazines.

Danny's mom stumbles onto his undesirable-food disposal system.

Long before he became famous as the host of "Jeopardy," Alex Trebek was a high school science teacher.

"Do you have any paper towels?!"

"Is she gone? Good. Her doctor just called and said she's a complete wacko. We're supposed to just give her a placebo prescription."

Prenatal peer pressure.

"Nurse Carlson has been suspended for two months. In the future, I suggest you refrain from chiding staff members about their weight."

Knowing that many passengers feel uneasy about flying, Mercury Airlines has installed simulated ground on all of its airliners.

"Oh, Lois, while you're here, I want to show you the needlepoint I'm working on. Now where the heck did I put it?"

"It gets worse. I called the customer service
number and it turns out to be
a video store in Guam."

The Fraziers opted for the deluxe
home security system.

"I must warn you, Ms. Maxwell,
I can read lips backward."

The Postal Service hits a grand slam
with its latest marketing ploy.

"Since you'll be baby-sitting for us on a regular basis, Tammy, we hope you won't object to having our pediatrician's phone number tattooed on your wrist."

"Oh, and Bill, listen to this! The red-kneed gargantua woodpecker is extremely rare, with confirmed sightings numbering fewer than fifty since 1900! How about that!"

The latest innovation for parents of toddlers: peel-away kitchen flooring.

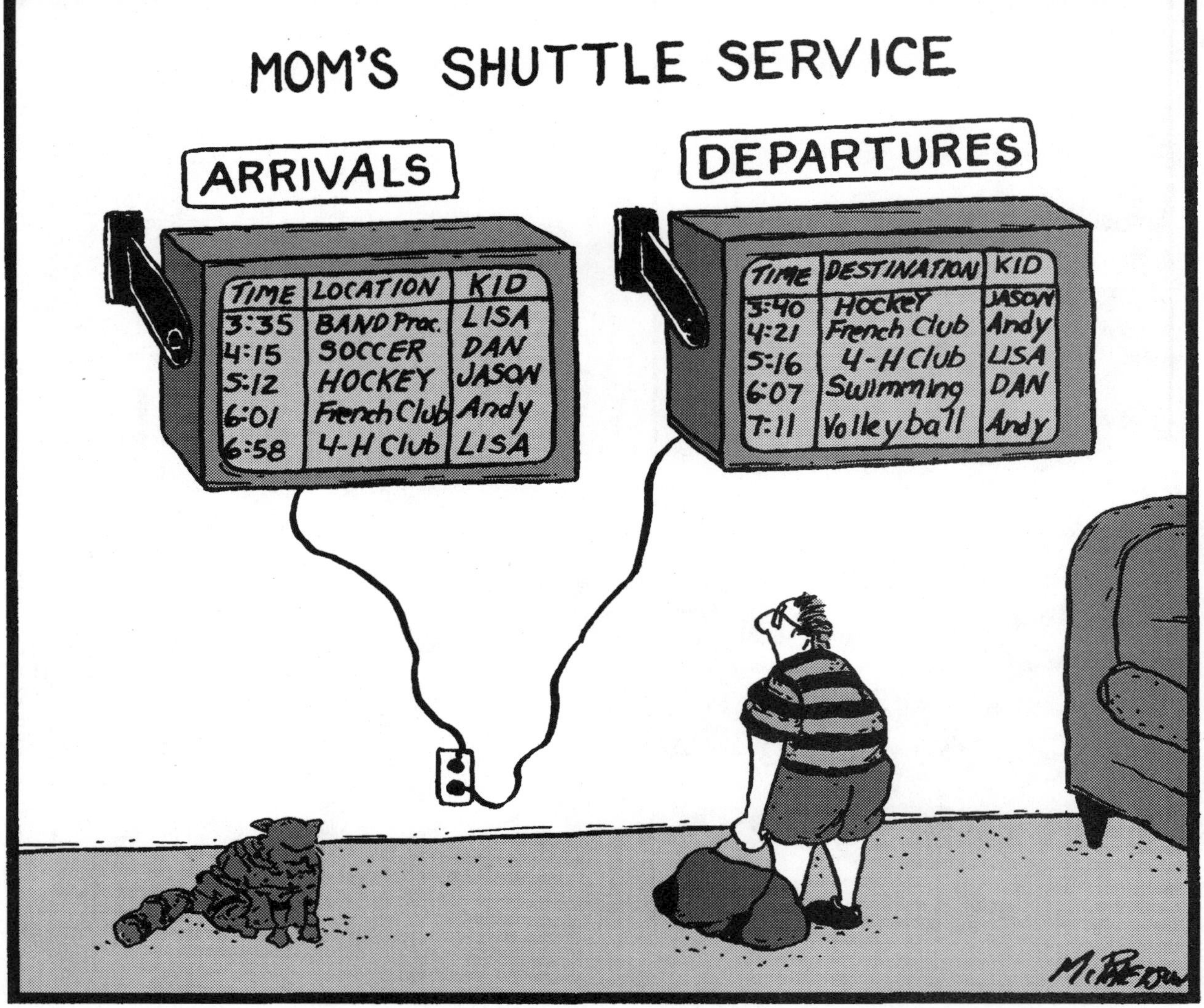
MOM'S SHUTTLE SERVICE
ARRIVALS
TIME LOCATION KID
3:35 BAND Prac. LISA
4:15 SOCCER DAN
5:12 HOCKEY JASON
6:01 French Club Andy
6:58 4-H Club LISA
DEPARTURES
TIME DESTINATION KID
3:40 Hockey JASON
4:21 French Club Andy
5:16 4-H Club LISA
6:07 Swimming DAN
7:11 Volleyball Andy

"I'm gonna have to charge you an extra three bucks for upholstery cleaning, sir."

"Yep! You were right! You do work better without dumb old me around!"

The Fettermans' mortgage officer goes over
their list of closing costs.

"Believe me, Mrs. Fansler, once we get finished,
your clogged tub days will be history!"

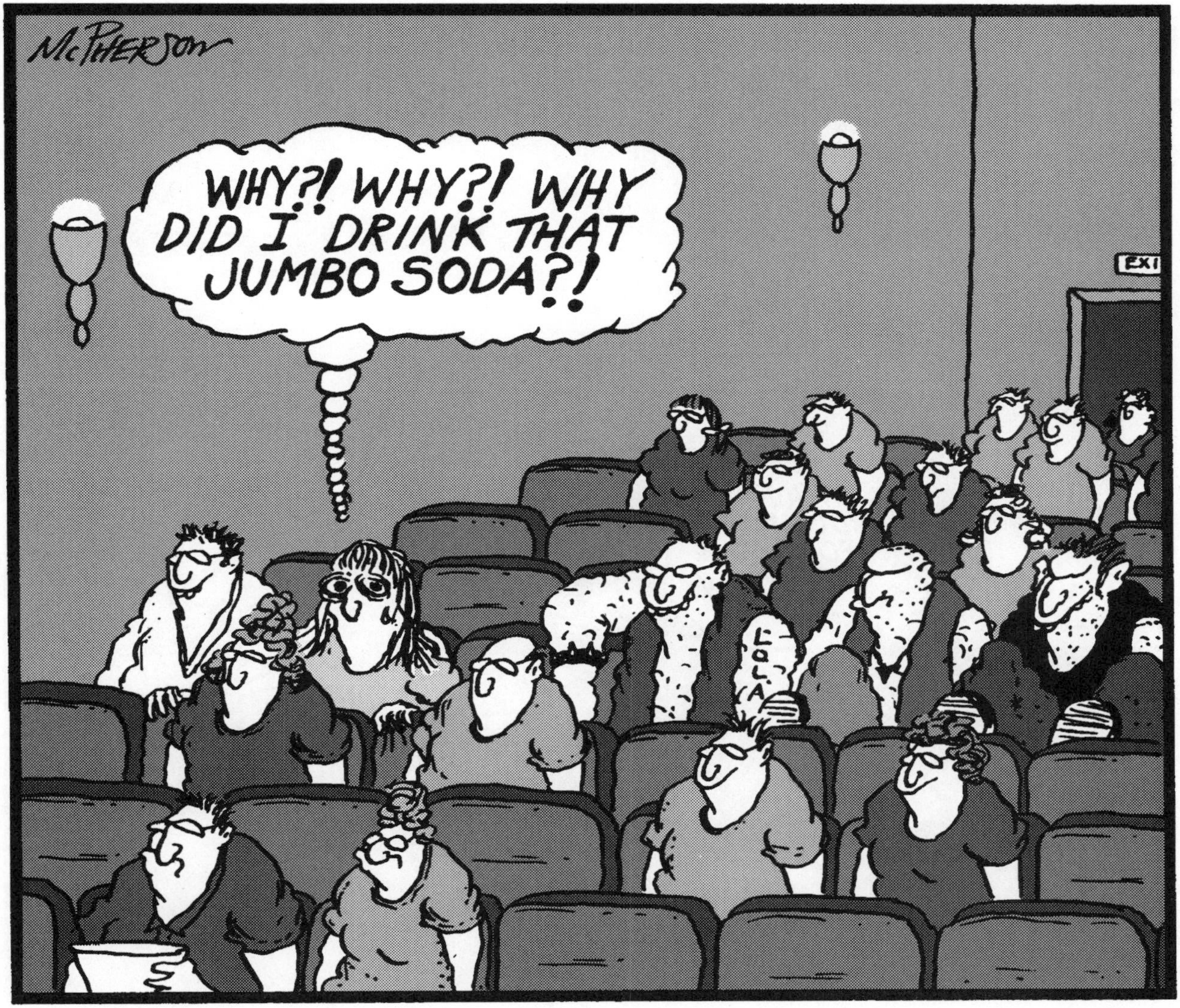
McPHERSON
WHY?! WHY?! WHY DID I DRINK THAT JUMBO SODA?!
EXI
LOLA

As Brad waited for his date, an excruciating silence fell over the room.